Featherstone

50

fantastic ideas for
physical activity outdoors

ALISTAIR BRYCE-CLEGG

Published 2013 by Featherstone Education
Bloomsbury Publishing plc
50 Bedford Square, London, WC1B 3DP

Bloomsbury is a registered trademark of Bloomsbury Publishing Plc

www.bloomsbury.com

ISBN 978-1-4081-8678-7

Text © Alistair Bryce-Clegg 2013
Design © Lynda Murray
Photographs © Shutterstock

Printed and bound in India by Replika Press Pvt.Ltd.

This book is produced using paper that is made from wood grown in
managed, sustainable forests. It is natural, renewable and recyclable.
The logging and manufacturing processes conform to the environmental
regulations of the country of origin.

10 9 8 7 6 5 4 3

To see our full range of titles visit **www.bloomsbury.com**

Acknowledgements
We would like to thank the staff and children of the following settings for their time
and patience in helping put this book together, including the use of a number of
photographs:

London Early Years Foundation, Emli Bendixen
Noah's Ark Pre-School
Marlborough Road Primary School
Sowe Valley Primary School
The Friars Primary School
Thorpedene Primary School

Also special thanks to Fee Bryce-Clegg

Contents

Introduction

The best sort of learning happens when children can mix education with fun. Their high level engagement in the task that they are doing will produce endless potential for high level attainment of learning. As educators of young children we not only have the fulfilling job of providing their constantly developing minds with exciting learning and information, but we also have a responsibility to help them develop the essential physical skills that they will need for success in their later lives.

The outdoors provide a fantastic opportunity for this sort of learning to happen. Children can get lost in their own little world of discovery as well as joining their friends by taking part in team games and shared learning.

In this book I have included activities for both individual play and group play. These activities will provide children with the opportunity to develop a range of skills from balance and coordination to gross and fine motor dexterity. Some of the activities are game based and will give children a chance to practise and rehearse social skills like turn taking, winning and losing! Some of the activities focus on the more creative aspects of learning in the outdoors by encouraging the children to make or build different structures. The children can then use what they have made or built in other aspects of their imaginative play.

The role of the adult in these activities very much depends on the age and physical dexterity of the children. Ideally the adult's role is to teach the children how to make, create or play in a way that enables and encourages them to use these new skills independently. The children can then take the structures, rules and ideas that they have helped create or been taught and invent new games or ways of working and playing with them.

This book will hopefully give you some new ideas to inspire you in your outdoor learning, which will in turn inspire some children in theirs!

Skin allergy alert

Some detergents and soaps can cause skin reactions.

Always be mindful of potential skin allergies when letting children mix anything with their hands and always provide lots of facilities to wash materials off after they have been in contact with the skin. Watch out for this symbol on the relevant pages.

Food allergy alert

When using food stuffs to enhance your outdoor play opportunities always be mindful of potential food allergies. We have used this symbol on the relevant pages.

Flags

What you need:

- 2 flags
- A hoop or skipping rope to make a jail

What to do:

1. Start by dividing the children into two teams.
2. Assign team one to the front of your outdoor area and team two to the back area.
3. The teams are given a limited time frame to hide their flag in their territory.
4. Once the flag is hidden, teams call out that they are finished.
5. They then must try and find the other team's flag.
6. If they get caught and tagged by an opponent on the opponent's territory they go to jail and can only be freed by a team mate who must grab them when their opponent isn't looking.
7. The first team to capture the flag or all of their opponents wins.

Taking it forward

- Add a challenge by increasing the number of flags that the children have to hide and retrieve.

What's in it for the children?

This is a great activity to get children moving around quickly to develop their fitness as well as their coordination and communication skills.

Five trees

What you need:

- **5 trees** (or large objects you can hide behind)

What to do:

1. Similar to hide-and-seek, 'five trees' is a game that needs to be played in an area that has at least five large trees in it.

2. Each tree is given a number from one to five.

3. The child who is 'in' stands with their back to the trees and counts to 20.

4. Each of the other players hides behind a tree so that they cannot be seen.

5. The player who is 'in' turns around and shouts out the number of a tree.

6. Anyone hiding behind that tree is then 'out'. Everyone else is safe.

7. The child who is 'in' turns around and counts to 20 again, while those still playing run and hide behind a different tree and so on, until there is only one hider left who then becomes the winner!

Taking it forward

- Add a challenge by increasing or reducing the amount of trees/ spaces that the children have to hide behind.

What's in it for the children?

This game is great for encouraging the children's ability to control their muscles and be still as well as opportunities to run and increase their fitness.

Balloon foot volleyball

What you need:

- Party balloons

What to do:

1. Set up the 'volleyball court' by putting a piece of string across the playing space, about 40cm off the ground.

2. Divide the players into two teams.

3. The two teams must lie on their backs with their feet in the air on either side of the string or 'net'.

4. Decide which team is going to go first. The first player must kick the balloon over the 'net'.

5. The teams must kick the balloon back and forth over the 'net' using only their feet and hands while lying on their backs.

6. If the balloon touches the floor, the team who missed it allows the other team to score one point.

7. The first team to reach 15 points wins.

Taking it forward

- Add a challenge by raising the height of the 'net'.

What's in it for the children?

Rather than using their upper body, this activity encourages the children to use their lower body and develop their coordination skills.

Outdoor bowling

What you need:

- Cereal boxes
- **A large ball** (football or sponge ball)
- Chalk or skipping rope for start line

What to do:

1. Line up the boxes in a row at least two metres away from the start line like bowling pins.

2. Use the ball to try to knock the 'pins' down.

3. For every 'pin' the players knock down, they are awarded one point.

4. Play as many rounds as you want.

5. The player who knocks down the most 'pins' is the winner.

Taking it forward

- Add a challenge by increasing the distance that the children stand from the pins and/or increase the number of the pins.

What's in it for the children?

This activity has lots of opportunities for children to develop their coordination and gross motor skills.

Sand pit golf

What you need:

- Buckets
- Spades
- Paper cups
- Shoe box
- Decorations such as mini flags, hoops, plastic toy etc.
- Stick, club or racquet
- A small ball

What to do:

1. Choose any part of your outdoor sand pit to build your course using your buckets and spades. The sand doesn't have to be flat to play sand pit golf, in fact it is more fun if there are lumps and bumps in the way!

2. Set up your course with features made from the paper cups and shoe boxes. You can cut the ends out of the shoe box and make a tunnel to hit your golf ball through. The cups can be used as a hazard too.

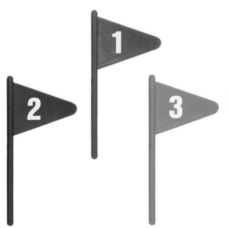

Taking it forward

- Add a challenge by increasing the number of cups and boxes that the children have to shoot their golf balls into or around.

What's in it for the children?

This activity is a great one for developing children's balance, hand/eye coordination and physical dexterity.

Batty hide and seek

What you need:

- Scissors
- Black craft paper
- Silver or gold ink pens or chalk
- Treasure

Turn left

What to do:

1. Cut out small bats from the black craft paper.
2. Write short clues on the bats in silver or gold pen that will lead your players from one place to the next.
3. Hide the bat clues in places that are not too easy to find!
4. Give the players the first clue and let them start their scavenger hunt.
5. The first player to reach the end is the winner of the treasure.

3 steps back

Taking it forward

- Add some physical challenges to your clues like 'do ten star jumps before you move on to the next clue'.

What's in it for the children?

The children will be using lots of physical skills as they search for and retrieve the clues.

Big ball relay

What you need:

- **A large ball** (such as sponge ball or beach ball)

What to do:

1. Line two teams up with the captain of each team standing about a metre away from the first person on their team.

2. To start the game, the captain throws the ball to the first player in the line who then throws the ball back and sits down.

3. The captain throws the ball to the next player, who throws the ball back and sits down behind the first person.

4. The captain continues in this way until all the players have had a turn.

5. When the last player catches the ball they then run to the captain to replace him, while the previous captain takes the position of first person in the line.

6. The new captain now repeats the throwing of the ball to each player.

7. The first team to have every player as the captain wins the game.

Taking it forward

■ Add a challenge by replacing the ball with a different shaped ball or a balloon.

What's in it for the children?

This activity is great for team work as well as developing throwing and catching skills.

Skipping splash

What you need:

- Paper cups
- Water
- Skipping rope or long rope

What to do:

1. Each player is given a cup of water.

2. Two people swing the skipping rope as each player takes turns to complete five to ten consecutive jumps while trying to keep as much water in their cup as possible.

3. The object of this game is to keep as much water in your cup as you can.

4. The last player with water in their cup wins.

Taking it forward

- Add a challenge by increasing the number of jumps in each round or providing a bigger cup of water.

What's in it for the children?

The children are getting the opportunity to develop balance, coordination and gross motor movement.

Catch an alien

What you need:

- **Strip of fabric** (to be used as the alien tail)

What to do:

1. The players sit on the ground in a circle.

2. One player remains standing and tucks the alien tail into their waistband. This player is the alien.

3. The alien circles the group, touching each player on the head saying, "Alien, alien!"

4. When the alien touches a player on the head and shouts, "Ben 10!" the alien has to run around the circle and take Ben 10's place before Ben 10 can grab the alien's tail.

5. If his tail is grabbed by Ben 10, then Ben 10 becomes the alien.

6. If the alien gets to Ben 10's place without being grabbed then he gets another turn at being the alien.

Taking it forward

- Add a challenge by giving your alien a shorter tail or increasing the size of the route that they have to run around to get back to their place.

What's in it for the children?

The children get the opportunity to develop their physical fitness as well as hand eye coordination and communication.

Tin can pyramid

What you need:

- **Tin cans**
- **Chalk**
- **A small ball** (like an airflow, hedgehog or sponge ball)

What to do:

1. Build a pyramid shape out of tin cans.

2. Using the chalk draw a line about a metre back from the pyramid of cans.

3. Challenge players to take turns to knock down the pyramid of cans. They can throw three balls per turn.

Taking it forward

- Add a challenge by moving the thrower further away from their target or by giving them a smaller ball.

What's in it for the children?

Children will have the opportunity to develop balance, gross motor movement, hand eye coordination and physical dexterity.

50 Fantastic Ideas for Physical Activity Outdoors

Freezing feet

What you need:

- Small pool or water tray
- Ice cubes
- Sunshine!

What to do:

1. Fill the pool with water and add ice cubes.

2. Each player has to remove the ice cubes with their feet and toes.

3. The player who removes the most ice cubes is the winner.

4. Make sure to do this activity on a sunny day so the children don't get too cold!

Taking it forward

- Add a challenge by putting larger pieces of ice in the tray and getting the children to sit down and use both feet to attempt to take the ice out.

What's in it for the children?

Apart from being great fun, this activity is good for encouraging children to develop their foot/eye coordination and dexterity. It also provides lots of opportunities for language development and talk.

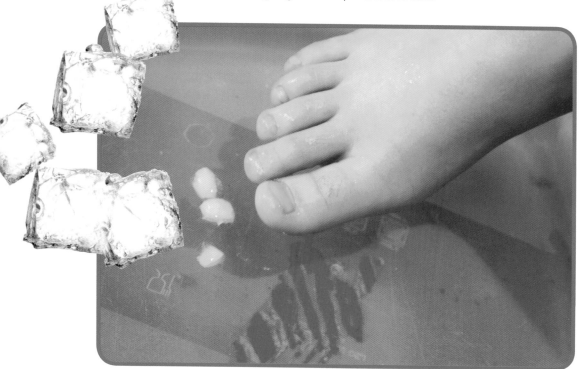

Fruit salad

What you need:

- Large indoor or outdoor space

What to do:

1. Get the children to form a circle.

2. Nominate a player to be 'in', that player stands in the centre of the circle.

3. Divide all players into three groups of fruit by going around the circle and naming them either apple, orange or pear.

4. The player who is 'in', calls the name of a fruit.

5. If he calls out apple, everyone who is that fruit must quickly change places with each other. Players who are not apples remain still.

6. The person who is 'in' tries to stand in a vacated space as the players swap positions.

7. If they manage to stand in a space then the player left at the end without a space stands in the centre of the circle and the game begins again.

8. The person in the middle can also call 'fruit salad' and everyone has to change places. The child that is then left without a place takes the role of being in the centre of the circle.

Taking it forward

- Add a challenge by getting the children to sit down for the entire game.

What's in it for the children?

The children are developing their gross motor skills as well as coordination and physical fitness.

I want my mummy!

What you need:

- **Strips of white fabric** (like an old bed sheet cut into strips), **toilet paper or bandages**
- **Timer or short piece of music**

What to do:

1. Divide the children into pairs.

2. One child plays the role of the 'mummy', while the other is the 'mummy wrapper'.

3. The aim of the game is to see which mummy wrapper can wrap their mummy in the fastest time.

Health & Safety

This should be a supervised activity. Make sure that children do not cover airways or wrap too tightly around the neck.

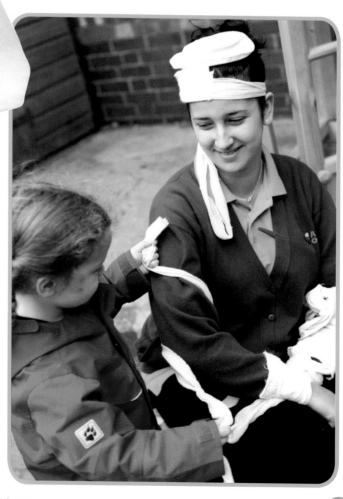

Taking it forward

- Add a challenge by getting the 'wrapper' to wear gloves or mitts when wrapping their mummy.

What's in it for the children?

This activity gives the children the opportunity to develop their fine motor skills and coordination.

Giant marbles

What you need:

- A skipping rope or string
- Chalk (if playing on a hard standing area)
- Lots of different sized balls

What to do:

1. Make a large circle with rope on grass or if you're on a hard standing area use chalk.

2. Place all the balls in the circle and spread them out a little.

3. Players take one ball and use this as the 'shooter'.

4. Standing two metres away from the edge of the circle, players take turns rolling their shooter at the balls inside the circle.

5. The aim is to try and knock as many balls as they can outside of the circle without the shooter going outside as well.

6. If a player manages to knock the balls outside of the circle (without his shooter going out), he keeps them and gets to have another turn.

7. When the circle is empty, the player with the most balls wins.

Taking it forward

- To add a challenge, make the circle bigger or the balls smaller.

What's in it for the children?

This is a brilliant activity for developing children's gross and fine motor skills as well as their hand/ eye coordination and aim.

Escaped from the zoo

What you need:

- Chalk, sticks or stones

What to do:

1. Using sticks, stones or chalk, mark out a large circle. This will be the 'zoo'.
2. Choose one player to be the zoo keeper and another to be the security guard.
3. The rest of the players take the role of the animals.
4. The guard must stay guarding the zoo for the duration of the game.
5. To start, the 'animals' run around as the zoo keeper tries to catch them. If the zoo keeper does catch one, they are lead over to the zoo.
6. Once in the zoo they cannot escape, but can be rescued if one of the other animals touches them.
7. The guard can chase away any prospective rescuers.
8. It is a good idea to set a time limit in advance or declare an end when a certain number of animals have been caught.

Taking it forward

- Add a challenge by having more than one zoo keeper or guard.

What's in it for the children?

This is a game that gets the children running about and therefore developing their levels of fitness. It also encourages them to use their communication skills as they plot their rescue.

Cat and mouse

What you need:

- Outdoor space

What to do:

1. Ask for two volunteers to play the cat and the mouse.

2. The other players form a circle and hold hands.

3. The player who is the mouse should stand inside of the circle while the cat remains outside of it.

4. The aim of the game is for the mouse to get outside of the circle and avoid being caught by the cat.

5. The mouse must stay moving while inside of the circle but cannot stay inside the circle for more than ten seconds.

6. The cat cannot come into the circle but they can reach into the circle to grab the mouse.

7. The players forming the circle have to try and keep the cat away from the mouse by holding up their hands to let the mouse in and out of the circle.

8. They can also block the cat's attempts to grab the mouse by standing in the cat's way.

9. If the mouse is caught, the mouse then takes the role of the cat.

10. The old cat joins the players holding hands and another player becomes the mouse.

Taking it forward

■ Add a challenge by increasing the number of cats or mice.

What's in it for the children?

This is a game of strategy as well as physical dexterity and coordination.

Get knotted

What you need:

- Large indoor or outdoor space

What to do:

1. Ask the children to stand in a circle with everyone facing inward.

2. Everyone stretches out their right hand into the middle of the circle and takes hold of someone else's hand.

3. Next they do the same with their left hands.

4. The object of the game is to see if they can untangle the 'knot' by stepping over or ducking under people, or turning around.

5. Whatever happens, they can't let go of each others hands!

Taking it forward

- Add a challenge by getting the children to sit down to start the game.

What's in it for the children?

This is a great game for developing coordination, gross motor movement and communication.

Bucket splash

What you need:

- Two chairs
- Two small buckets
- Two plastic cups
- One large bucket
- Warm water

What to do:

1. In an outside space divide the players into two teams.

2. Nominate a player from each team to sit on a chair away from the rest of their team members.

3. Give the seated players a plastic bucket each to hold on their head.

4. Give one player in each team a small plastic cup.

5. Place a bucket of warm water half way between the teams and the seated players with the buckets on their head.

6. The player with the cup from each team must run to their bucket, fill their cup and carefully run and pour it into the plastic bucket on their seated player's head, trying not to spill any water as they run.

7. When the player returns to their team they pass the cup to the next player who then repeats the filling activity.

8. Continue like this until the bucket has been filled up.

9. The first team to fill their bucket is the winner.

Taking it forward

- Add a challenge by using bottles and funnels instead of buckets.

What's in it for the children?

This is a great activity for developing team work, communication, coordination and fitness.

Three-legged tights race

What you need:
- Several pairs of tights
- Start and finish line

What to do:
1. Ask the children to find a friend and make a pair.
2. Give each pair of children one pair of tights.
3. Ask them each to put their opposite leg into the same leg of a pair of tights.
4. Once their legs are together in the tights leg, the children race to the finish line.

Taking it forward
- Add a challenge by increasing the distance that the children have to run.

What's in it for the children?
This is a great activity for developing coordination and cooperation as well as fitness.

Water balloon toss

What you need:
- Party balloons
- Water

What to do:
1. Pre-fill your balloons with water.
2. Ask the children to form a circle and to pass a balloon around the circle slowly.
3. Get faster and faster as the game goes on.
4. The game ends when someone drops the balloon and it explodes!

Taking it forward
- Add a challenge by covering the filled balloons in baby oil or have two balloons moving around the circle in opposite directions.

What's in it for the children?

The children get the opportunity to develop their gross motor skills as well as coordination.

Chinese ball

What to do:

1. Children stand in a circle with a ball that is appropriate for the age group.

2. The ball is thrown quickly around and across the circle.

3. As soon as a child catches the ball, the children on either side of him must raise one arm - the arm nearest the child with the ball - and hold it in the air until the ball is passed on to another child.

4. If a child fails to catch the ball, is too slow to pass the ball along or fails to raise the correct arm when their neighbour catches the ball, they drop out.

5. When there are only five children left in the circle, they are all declared winners, and the game starts again.

Taking it forward

- Add a challenge by having two balls being bounced around the circle.

What's in it for the children?

The children are getting the opportunity to develop their sense of balance and physical awareness. They also need good coordination skills to get the correct arm in the air at the correct time.

Mr Troll, Mr Troll

What you need:

- A copy of the *Three Billy Goats Gruff* (optional)

What to do:

1. Select one person to be the troll who will then stand in the center of the playing area.

2. The other children stand approximately 150 feet from him.

3. The children shout, "Mr Troll, Mr Troll, may we cross your bridge?"

4. He answers by saying, "Only if you are..." and describes something worn by one or more players. For example, he might say, "You can cross only if you are wearing blue socks." Or, "If you have glasses."

5. Anyone wearing blue socks runs across the playing area towards the finish line, trying to avoid the troll who tags as many players as possible.

6. Tagged players become trolls and help catch other goats.

7. The game ends when everybody has been caught.

Taking it forward

- Add a challenge by increasing the size of the playing area to make it harder for the trolls to catch their goats!

What's in it for the children?

The children are developing their gross motor skills and fitness by running. They are also developing their hand/eye and physical coordination skills if they are the catcher.

Hula hoop hoot

What you need:

- A hula hoop

What to do:

1. Place a hula hoop over one child's arm and then get all of the children to join hands to make a circle.

2. The children have to move the hoop around the circle without letting go of each other's hands.

Taking it forward

- Add a challenge by having two hoops and send them around the circle in opposite directions.

What's in it for the children?

This helps the children develop their balance and coordination as well as communication skills.

Space race relay

What you need:

- Space hoppers
- Chalk or skipping rope for start and finish line

What to do:

1. Blow up your space hoppers.

2. Divide the children into two teams.

3. Divide each team up again, placing them at either end of your space race track.

4. The first child from each team bounces down the track. When they reach the other end they swap with one of their team members waiting on that side.

5. When all team members have had a turn, that team has won.

Taking it forward

- Add a challenge by making the course longer.

What's in it for the children?

Managing to stay on a space hopper requires balance and muscle control. Bouncing forward on one exercises the muscles in the legs as well as raising the heart rate for general fitness.

Digging for treasure

What you need:

- Outdoor sand pit or digging pit
- Spades
- Buckets
- Timer
- **Treasure** (plastic coins, gem stones etc.)

What to do:

1. Bury your treasure in advance so that the children cannot see where you have put it.
2. Give the children a spade to dig with and a bucket or container to collect their treasure in.
3. Set the timer and let the children dig.
4. The child who collects the most treasure in the time given is the winner.
5. Let the children bury the treasure that they have found for the next group who come along.

Taking it forward

- Add a challenge by burying the treasure deeper in the sand and/ or by giving the children smaller utensils to dig with.

What's in it for the children?

The physical motion of large scale digging helps the children to build strength in their upper body as well as supporting the development of their balance and hand/eye coordination.

Sneaky bear

What you need:

- A blanket
- 3 or more objects to hide
- Teddy bear (optional)

What to do:

1. Get the children to hide under the blanket and 'go to sleep'.
2. You or a child, or group of children then hide the objects in your outdoor area.
3. Tell the children under the blanket to 'wake up' as Sneaky Bear has taken and hidden their belongings.
4. The game is over when the children find all of the hidden objects.

Taking it forward

- Add a challenge by increasing the number of objects that are hidden.

What's in it for the children?

This activity encourages the children to use their entire body to search for the hidden objects. Depending on the size of the space that they are searching in, it can also support general fitness and exercise.

Hungry caterpillar hopscotch

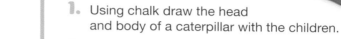

What you need:

- Playground chalk
- Stone or counter
- Copy of *The Very Hungry Caterpillar* (optional)

What to do:

1. Using chalk draw the head and body of a caterpillar with the children.

2. Make sure that the caterpillar's body is very 'wiggly' and not just in a straight line!

3. Number each of the circles that make the caterpillar's body.

4. Ask the children to throw their counter onto the caterpillar's body and hop to where it lands.

Taking it forward

- Add a picture of the food that the caterpillar ate on each day to the circles and get the children to shout it out when they land on it. You could also make the caterpillar even longer for a bigger hopping challenge.

What's in it for the children?

Hopping is good for the children's balance and coordination as well as being a good form of exercise.

No snow snowball throw

What you need:

- **Tights** (light colour)
- **Cotton wool or toy stuffing**

Taking it forward

- Add a challenge to the activity by introducing a target to aim the snowballs at or a minimum distance for them to be thrown.

What's in it for the children?

While the children are throwing and catching they will be supporting the development of their balance and gross motor movement as well as hand eye coordination.

What to do:

1. Cut the legs of each pair of tights into 10cm sections.
2. Tie or stitch one end.
3. Stuff with cotton wool or toy stuffing.
4. Tie or stitch the other end.
5. Shape into a ball.
6. Go and throw your snowballs!

Tree stump climb

What you need:

- Tree or tree stump
- Pack of climbing wall holds (grips)
- Screwdriver
- Screws

What to do:

1. Attach your climbing wall holds to the circumference of your tree or tree stump a little way off the ground. You will need to do two rows, one for the children's hands and another for their feet.

2. Do not put climbing wall holds above the height that you want the children to climb to.

3. The children can then climb around the tree as often as they like!

Taking it forward

- You can attach climbing wall holds to multiple trees and create a mini assault course. If you haven't got any trees in your outdoor space, or they are not big enough then you can also attach climbing wall holds to an outdoor wall.

What's in it for the children?

Climbing is great for coordination and muscle development.

Big bucket bonanza

What you need:

- **Large and small buckets**
- **Selection of other containers**
- **Plastic tubing**
- **Guttering**
- **Construction** (such as milk crates or bread crates)
- **Access to water** (such as a hosepipe)
- **Waterproof clothing and footwear** (optional)

What to do:

1. Allow the children to experiment with the movement of large volumes of water.

2. Children should have the opportunity to fill and empty both large and small containers.

3. Children should also be encouraged to construct structures that will transport their water over large distances and allow them to collect it again, for example by using the guttering.

Health & Safety

Make sure that children are supervised when working with large volumes of water.

Taking it forward

- To add challenge to this activity you can vary the range and size of resources that you provide to support the play.

What's in it for the children?

This type of large scale construction requires the children to lift and stretch. The weight of the water will also provide some resistance and offer opportunities of the development of their upper body alongside balance and coordination.

Close shave

What to do:

1. Squirt the shaving foam into the paint trays.
2. Use the rollers to apply the shaving foam to the tree.
3. Turn the lolly stick onto its side and use it to 'shave' the tree.
4. You have to be quick before the shaving foam disappears!

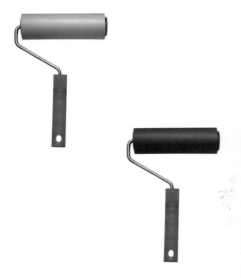

Taking it forward

- To add some challenge increase the number or the size of the trees that you are shaving.
- Assign trees to the children and see who can shave their tree the fastest!

What's in it for the children?

In the application of the foam with the roller, the children are reaching and stretching. Because they have to be quick they will be increasing their heart rate which could help improve their fitness.

Painting with tights

What you need:

- **Plastic containers** (such as ice cream tubs)
- **Paint**
- **Large paper** (such as lining paper)
- **Pair of tights**
- **Cotton wool**

What to do:

1. Fill your plastic containers with paint.
2. Roll out your paper along the ground.
3. Cut off one leg from a pair of tights.
4. Put a large ball of 'damp' cotton wool into the foot of the tight.
5. Holding the other end of the tight, dip the cotton wool stuffed foot into the paint.
6. Keeping a tight hold, swing your arm over your head and 'splat' the paint onto your paper!

Taking it forward

- To add a challenge to this activity cut your tights to different lengths.

- Try attaching paper to a tree or wall so that the children have to use different body movements to achieve their 'splat' artwork.

What's in it for the children?

This activity encourages the development of balance and coordination as well as upper body movement and dexterity.

Painting with mops

What you need:

- Paint
- Plastic containers (big enough to fit the mop head into)
- Washing up liquid
- Mops
- Large pieces of paper (such as wall paper or lining paper)

What to do:

1. Put your paint into the plastic containers and spread out your paper on the ground.

2. Add a squirt of washing up liquid to each container of paint, this helps the mop to move along the paper. (If you want to save on the amount of paint that you are using then add some water at this stage and mix well).

3. Dip the mops into the paint and get painting!

Taking it forward

- To increase the challenge for this activity, get the children to mop over a larger distance or increase the speed at which they mop by asking them to cover a specific area within a given time.

What's in it for the children?

This activity encourages the development of balance and coordination as well as upper body movement and dexterity.

Making tracks

What you need:

- Scissors
- Skewer
- Plastic milk cartons (various sizes)
- Dry sand

What to do:

1. Use the skewer or scissors to pierce holes into the lid or bottom of your milk cartons **(adult only)**.

2. Vary the number and size of the holes in each carton.

3. Fill the cartons with sand.

4. Get some children to make tracks for the others to follow by pouring the sand out of their cartons through the holes.

Health & Safety

Make sure that the skewer is only used safely by a responsible adult and kept out of reach of children.

Taking it forward

- To encourage the children to move quickly make the holes in your carton large so that the sand comes out fast.

What's in it for the children?

There is lots of movement involved in this activity involving all parts of the body. It will support the children in the development of their coordination and balance as well as their general fitness.

Swing ball tights

What you need:

- **A pair of tights**
- **Balls** (tennis balls are quite good in this activity)
- **Tennis racquet**
- **Washing line**
- **Pegs**

What to do:

1. Cut the legs off your pair of tights.
2. Drop a ball into the foot of each leg.
3. Tie or peg the open end of the leg securely to a washing line.
4. Take aim and hit it with your tennis racquet!

Taking it forward

■ You can add challenge to this activity by swapping the tennis racquet for a smaller bat.

What's in it for the children?

This activity is great for supporting the children in the development of their hand/eye coordination as well as their balance and upper body movement.

Den making

What you need:

- Washing line
- Cardboard boxes
- Milk and bread crates
- Pegs
- Fabric
- Carpet inner tubes
- Tarpaulin

What to do:

1. Start by creating a structure for your den using the washing line, boxes and crates.

2. Then drape, peg or tie all of the fabric and various materials provided to create your shelter.

Taking it forward

- Add challenge to this activity by increasing the size or changing the shape of your structure. Also try introducing a different range of resources for the children to build with.

What's in it for the children?

This activity encourages the children to use their upper body dexterity as well as balance and coordination.

Natural den making

What you need:

- A selection of natural materials such as sticks, leaves, twigs, string

What to do:

1. Collect your natural materials together.

2. Find a suitable support (like a tree or bush).

3. Work with the materials you have found to create a shelter that children could sit inside.

Health & Safety

When working with natural materials, always ensure that suitable risk assessments are in place.

Taking it forward

- Add challenge to this activity by increasing the size or changing the shape of your structure.

What's in it for the children?

This activity encourages the children to use their upper body dexterity as well as balance and coordination.

Giant water bag

What you need:

- Large rectangular piece of builder's plastic
- Strong gaffer tape
- Hose pipe

What to do:

1. Take your rectangular sheet of builder's plastic and fold it in half.

2. Tape both sides to the ground using strong gaffer tape until it looks like a giant sleeping bag!

3. Tape across the remaining open end, leaving a small hole to insert the hose.

4. Fill the big bag with water.

5. Once you feel there is enough water in the bag tape up the remaining hole.

6. Lie it flat on the ground and play (always best to remove your shoes!)

Taking it forward

■ Add a challenge to this activity by introducing different resources to encourage physical development like balls for throwing and catching.

What's in it for the children?

This activity encourages the children to use their bodies in different ways. They will have the opportunity to lie down, stretch and roll.

Trail making

What you need:

- Twigs
- Leaves
- Stones
- Grass

What to do:

1. Using natural materials you are going to create a trail of symbols for the children to follow.

2. First explain to the children what each symbol means. An arrow made of twigs will tell them which direction to go in. Four stones in a box will tell them how many steps to take. A leaf under a stone will tell them to look down. A leaf on top of a stone will tell them to look up.

3. Next lay out your trail and invite the children to follow it!

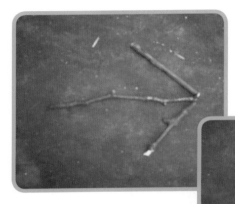

Taking it forward

- Add a challenge to this activity by increasing the length and complexity of your trail.

- Once your children have got the idea of what to do, encourage them to come up with trails of their own.

What's in it for the children?

Depending on how long or how complex the trail is, the physical challenge for the children is going to be different. They will have the opportunity to develop their coordination skills alongside gross and fine motor dexterity.

Ramps and ledges

What you need:

- Hollow wooden blocks
- Planks
- Milk crates
- Bread crates

What to do:

1. Work with the children to build structures that will encourage them to travel, move around and use their bodies in different ways.

2. Use the blocks and crates to create height and the planks to create ramps.

Taking it forward

- Add a challenge to this activity by increasing the size or complexity of the structure that you build.

- Try introducing other resources or game based play.

What's in it for the children?

Children will be using lots of physical skills both in the creation and the use of this activity. They will have the opportunity to travel using different parts of their body using balance alongside gross and fine motor dexterity.

Archaeological dig

What you need:

- Treasures to bury such as: bones, coins, gem stones, pottery
- Trowels
- Buckets/bags for finds
- **Paint brushes** (optional – for dusting finds)
- **Washing up bowl with warm water** (optional for washing finds)
- Maps, paper, pencils

What to do:

1. Bury your archaeological finds.
2. Explain to the children what an archaeological dig is.
3. Let the children dig and discover.
4. The children can clean, record and store what they discover.

Taking it forward

- For a more physical challenge (for you and the children) you can bury your archaeological finds a bit deeper.

What's in it for the children?

The children will have the opportunity to develop their coordination skills alongside balance and upper body dexterity.

Muddy puddle grab

What you need:

- A muddy puddle
- Airflow balls in two or more colours (depending on the number of children playing.)
- Litter pickers or grab sticks
- Timer
- Container to collect your balls in

What to do:

1. Make a puddle by digging a hole and pouring water into it.
2. Drop all of the balls into the puddle and give them a good mix.
3. Set the timer.
4. Assign a different colour to each child and using the litter pickers get them to pick up their colour of balls.
5. The child who picks up all of their colour of balls first before the timer runs out is the winner.

Taking it forward

- To add a challenge to this activity, increase the amount of balls or reduce the time the children have to grab them.

What's in it for the children?

This activity is good for developing hand eye coordination, balance as well as fine and gross motor skills.

Chicken hop

What you need:

- Each player needs 10 sticks, each about 30cm long

What to do:

1. Lay your sticks on the ground like a ladder roughly 25cm apart with one ladder for each player.

2. Hop over the sticks on one leg without touching any of them. If a stick is touched, then you are out.

3. When you have hopped over all of the sticks you stop, still on one leg, bend down and pick up the last stick. Then hop back over the remaining sticks.

4. When you get to the beginning again, drop the stick you have picked up and set off again to hop over the nine remaining sticks, pick up the last one, and come back again.

5. Keep going until all of the sticks are picked up.

6. The first child to pick up all of the sticks is the winner.

7. If your children are too young to hop do it by jumping with their feet together.

Taking it forward

- You can add a challenge to this activity by making the gap in between the sticks smaller or by adding more sticks

What's in it for the children?

This game is great for balance and coordination, not to mention hopping!

outdoor twister

What you need:

- **Ready mix paint in 4 colours** (if you are playing on grass)
- **Chalk in 4 colours** (if you are playing on a hard surface)
- **Paint brush**

What to do:

1. You need to create a row of six circles of each colour. Each circle should be approximately 10cm apart from the one next to it and also 10cm away from the one above/below it.

2. To make a paint circle, lay your plate on the grass, paint around the outside, lift up your plate and then fill in the centre.

3. To make a chalk circle do the same as paint, only with your chalk!

4. One child or adult calls out left or right, followed by 'hand' or 'foot' followed by one of the colours that you have painted your circles. All players have to follow the instruction at the same time or they are out.

Taking it forward

- For more of a stretch you can move your circles further apart.

What's in it for the children?

This is a great game for encouraging balance, coordination and muscle control.

Build a brick wall

What you need:

- Cement
- 2 x sheets of hardboard or cardboard
- Bricks
- Trowel
- Water

What to do:

1. Mix the cement on one of your sheets of hardboard (to save the condition of your outdoor surface).
2. Place the bricks on your other sheet of hardboard.
3. Cement subsequent rows together using the cement and trowel.

Taking it forward

- This is a great activity to do with children where the adult can very much take the lead. The children can then replicate the skills that they have experienced in their play.

- Instead of cement try using very thick mud or sand and PVA glue which can be mixed in the same way.

What's in it for the children?

This activity will support children's hand/eye coordination, upper body coordination and balance.

Tyre rolling

What you need:

- Tyres of various sizes
- Open space
- As varied a landscape as possible

What to do:

1. Essentially you are just going to roll the tyres, but the possibilities of how or where you roll them are endless.

2. Try rolling your tyre on a flat surface and keeping it in a straight line.

3. Try rolling your tyre down a slope or hill and controlling its speed with your hands.

4. You can roll your tyre down a slope, giving it a head start and then try to catch up with it.

Taking it forward

- Different sizes of tyres will present different challenges.

- You can also introduce more levels of challenge by asking the children to move their tyre around a particular route or move it in a particular way.

What's in it for the children?

Managing the shape and weight of a tyre will help children to develop upper body strength as well as balance and coordination. Chasing or running with their tyre will increase their heart rate, which in turn will impact on their fitness.

Welly wanging

What you need:

- Several wellington boots
- A skipping rope

What to do:

1. Lay a skipping rope on the floor as your 'wanging' start line.

2. Ask the children to throw their welly as far as they can.

3. The child who 'wangs' their welly the furthest is the winner.

Health & Safety

Make sure children have appropriate space both in front and behind them when they throw.

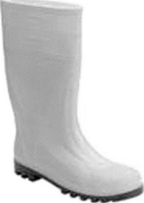

Taking it forward

- To add some challenge to this activity give the children bigger wellies to throw.

What's in it for the children?

This activity supports children in their development of their balance, hand/eye coordination, gross motor movement and upper body strength.

Who's got the beanbag?

Taking it forward

■ The number the children count up to depends on the size of the circle. The number can also change with each game. The beanbag can be substituted for a smaller item like a ball or a button for older children or children with greater dexterity.

What's in it for the children?

This activity is great for supporting the children in the development of their senses and concentration. They have to count out loud whilst manipulating an object that they cannot see.

What to do:

1. The children stand in a circle with their shoulders touching.

2. One child stands in the middle of the circle.

3. The rest of the children standing in the circle pass the beanbag around behind their backs.

4. Those without the beanbag pretend to pass it.

5. As the beanbag is being passed the children count out loud and in unison.

6. When they get to a predetermined number they stop passing the beanbag.

7. When the passing stops, the player in the middle has to guess as to who actually has the beanbag.

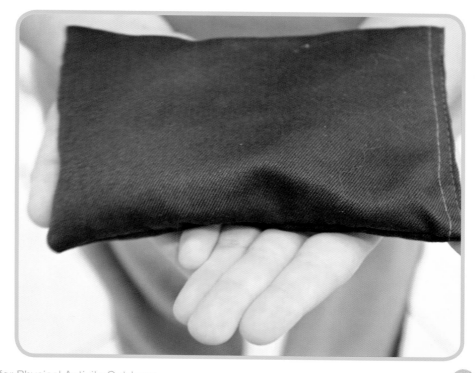

Spaghetti fling painting

What you need:

- Paper
- Cooked spaghetti
- Paint
- Plastic containers for paint (ice cream tub size)

What to do:

1. Spread the paper out on the ground.
2. Children dip the cooked spaghetti into the paint.
3. They fling the painted spaghetti at the paper.
4. Either lift or shake the spaghetti off and start again.

50 Fantastic Ideas for Physical Activity Outdoors

Taking it forward

- Add some challenge to this activity by making the paper bigger so that the children fling the spaghetti even further using their shoulder joints as well as their elbows.

What's in it for the children?

Any activity that involves throwing is good for developing balance, coordination and upper body dexterity.

50 Fantastic Ideas for Physical Activity Outdoors

Shift the stick

What you need:

- Chalk
- A stick
- Bean bags

Taking it forward

- To add a challenge to this game make the teams stand even further away from the chalk lines.

What's in it for the children?

This is a great game for balance and coordination. Children will be using their upper body strength and hand/eye coordination to try and hit the stick with their beanbag.

What to do:

1. This game can be played by two players or by two teams.

2. Draw two parallel lines with the chalk about two metres apart.

3. Lay a stick in between the two chalk lines so that it is parallel to them.

4. The children stand opposite each other behind the lines and take turns throwing beanbags at the stick to try and move it across the opposing teams line.

5. The first child or team to get the stick over their opponents' line is the winner.